REMARKABLE CHILDREN

Maria de Sautuola

THE BULLS IN THE CAVE

A Picture-Book Biography

The information for the Remarkable Children Series was

gathered from old letters, journals, and other historical documents.

For Diana Judith Fradin, From Dad, With Love.
D.F.
To My Parents, Gabriel and Nelly
E.M.

The author thanks Maria de Sautuola's son,
Emilio Botin, for providing many details about her life.

Text copyright ©1997 by Dennis Fradin
Illustrations copyright © 1997 by Ed Martinez
Photo credits: Photo Research by Susan Van Etten Photo Research; p. 32, all, ©Douglas Mazonowicz/ Gallery of Prehistoric Art; back cover, courtesy of Emilio Botin.

Published by Silver Press
A Division of Simon & Schuster
299 Jefferson Road, Parsippany, NJ 07054

Designed by Brooks Design

Printed in the United States of America

ISBN 0-382-39470-4 (LSB) 10 9 8 7 6 5 4 3 2 1
ISBN 0-382-39471-2 (PBK) 10 9 8 7 6 5 4 3 2 1

Library of Congress Cataloging-in-Publication Data

Fradin, Dennis B.
Maria de Sautuola: the bulls in the cave/by Dennis Fradin: illustrated by Ed Martinez.
p. cm.—(Remarkable children series: #2)
Summary: The true story of Maria de Sautuola, an eight-year-old Spanish girl who discovered the first known prehistoric cave paintings in 1879 while working with her father in Altamira Cave.
1. Altamira Cave (Spain)—Juvenile literature. 2. Paleolithic period—Spain—Cantabria—Juvenile literature. 3. Cave paintings—Spain—Cantabria—Juvenile literature. 4.Sautuola, Maria de, b. 1870—Juvenile literature. 5. Children—Spain—Cantabria—Biography. 6. Sautuola, Marcelino Sanz de, 1831-1888—Juvenile literature. 7. Excavations (Archaeology)—Spain—Cantabria—Juvenile literature. 8. Cantabria (Spain)—Antiquities—Juvenile literature. (1. Sautuola, Maria de. b. 1870. 2. Sautuola, Marcelino Sanz de, 1831-1888. 3. Altamira Cave (Spain) 4. Cave paintings. 5. Art, Prehistoric.)
I. Martinez, Ed. ill. II. Title. III. Series.
GN772.22.S7F73 1996
936.6—dc20 96-5027(B) CIP AC

REMARKABLE CHILDREN

Maria de Sautuola

THE BULLS IN THE CAVE

The true story of an eight-year-old Spanish girl who discovered the first known prehistoric cave paintings in 1879.

BY DENNIS FRADIN • ILLUSTRATED BY ED MARTINEZ

Silver Press

Parsippany, New Jersey

Maria de Sautuola was born in northern Spain on November 30, 1870. She was the only child of a wealthy nobleman and his wife who owned an estate near the city of Santander. The mountainous area where the Sautuolas' estate was located was known as Altamira, meaning "High View."

Shortly before Maria's birth, a hunting dog discovered a cave on the Sautuolas' property—although it may be more accurate to say that the cave found the dog. The animal was roaming the countryside with its master when suddenly it disappeared in a crack in a hillside. As the hunter rescued his barking dog, he saw that the crack was actually a cave opening that had been covered by dirt and twigs. The hunter told Maria's father, Don Marcelino de Sautuola, about the cave on his property. Don Marcelino had little interest at first, for the mountains of northern Spain had many caves. Not until 1875, when Maria was five years old, did Don Marcelino clear the debris from the entrance and explore the cave a little.

In 1877 Maria's father made a trip to Paris, France. There he attended a convention of archaeologists—

scientists who study the remains of past human cultures. The scientists were excited about some skeletons that had recently been found in the Cro-Magnon Cave in France. The skeletons belonged to a prehistoric people who looked much like us and who lived scattered about Europe, Asia, and Africa between 40,000 and 10,000 years ago. These prehistoric relatives of ours were named the Cro-Magnon, for the cave in which their remains were first found. Don Marcelino wondered: Might Cro-Magnon people have lived in the cave on his property thousands of years ago?

After returning home from Paris, Don Marcelino began to dig inside his cave near the entrance. Since it was lonely work, he asked Maria to keep him company. The six-year-old girl with short brown hair and lively brown eyes was happy to help her father. She held the candles so that he could see where to dig. And sometimes he held the candles so that she could scoop out a little dirt with her small shovel.

Notes made by Don Marcelino reveal that within a year or so, he and his daughter had dug down to a depth of 12 inches (30 centimeters). They had

discovered dozens of relics left by the Cro-Magnon people. The piles of wild animals' bones and teeth that they found showed that the cave dwellers had been hunters. The shells from oysters and other sea creatures proved that they had visited the nearby seashore. Maria and her father also uncovered stone tools and a few pieces of clay pottery. Maria felt proud to help her father with something so important, for to him each new discovery of a scraping tool or a spearpoint was like finding a diamond or a gold nugget.

Maria and her father always did their digging near the cave entrance, where the ancient people had lived. As the months passed, Maria grew curious about the passages to the rear of the cave, which she and her father had never entered. She wanted to ask him if she could go by herself to look around, but each time she stared into the darkness, she changed her mind.

One summer day in 1879, Maria and her father went with their candles and shovels to the cave on the hillside. As they dug in their usual spot, Maria again began to wonder about the back of the cave. This time she did not let her fear overcome her curiosity. Maria

asked her father if she could go deeper into the cave by herself. Don Marcelino answered yes, warning her to be careful.

The eight-year-old girl took a candle and began walking slowly through the passage. With each step, she had to fight the urge to run back to her father, for the strange dancing shapes cast by the candle's flame seemed to leap out at her from the walls and ceiling. Yet Maria continued, step by step, until finally she entered a great hall of the cave.

Maria explored the huge chamber for a few moments. Then something caught her eye that caused her to scream *"Toros! Toros!"* meaning "Bulls! Bulls!" There on the ceiling, above her head, were many beautiful paintings of animals. In the flickering light, they appeared to be running across the ceiling, and their eyes seemed to be staring down at her.

Don Marcelino couldn't imagine how bulls had entered the cave, but as his daughter's shouts echoed through the halls and tunnels, he didn't waste a second. He ran toward Maria with his shovel to protect her. He found her in the large hall gazing up in wonderment at

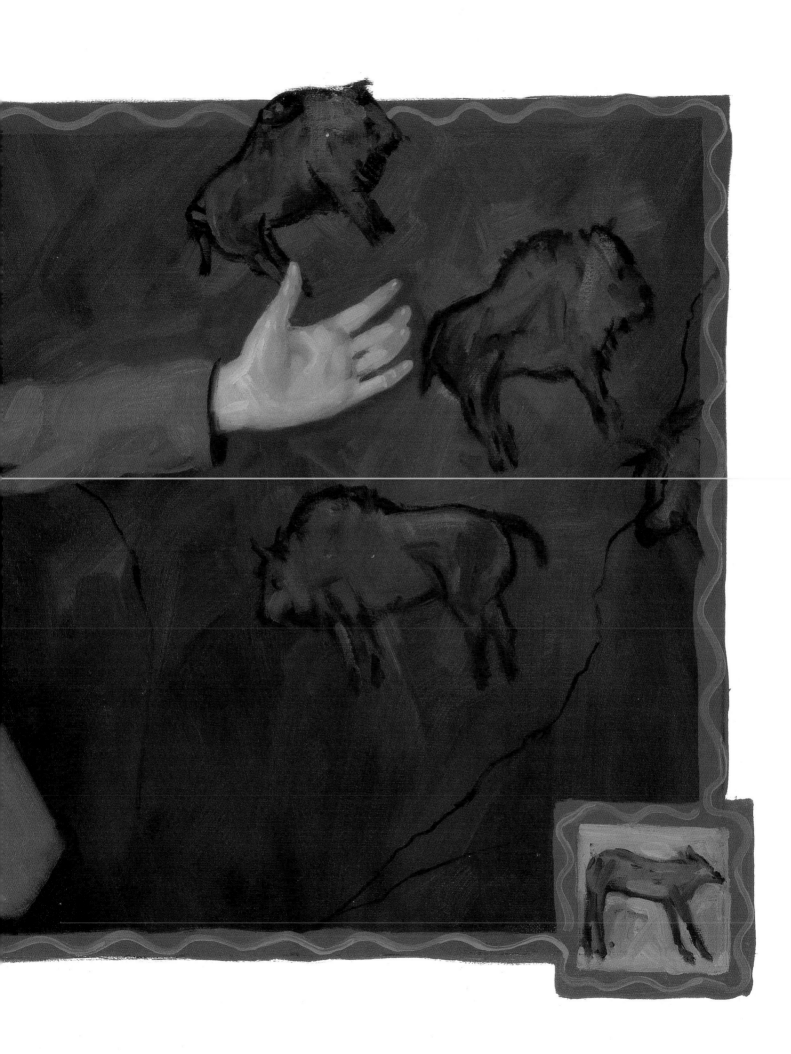

some of the most beautiful paintings of animals he had ever seen. The animals she had thought were bulls were really bison. Also on the cave ceiling were graceful paintings of deer, horses, wild boars, and a wolf.

Maria's father said that he believed prehistoric people had painted the pictures and that she had made a tremendous discovery. When she asked why the paint looked so fresh, he answered that the cave had been sealed for thousands of years, protecting the pictures from the air. However, scientists would have to study the paintings to make certain of their age.

Don Marcelino wrote letters to several scientists, inviting them to visit the cave. One of them, Professor Juan de Vilanova y Piera of Madrid, agreed to come. On the day that the professor arrived from Spain's capital city, Don Marcelino and Maria led him out to their cave. The professor looked up at the ceiling in astonishment and then said that Maria had made a discovery of the utmost importance. She had found the first known cave paintings created by ancient people. Professor Vilanova figured that the paintings were about 15,000 years old, which was the actual

fact. As a clue to the great age of the cave art, he pointed to the bison. These animals hadn't existed in Spain for more than 12,000 years.

But Maria had found far more than the world's oldest known paintings, the professor continued. Archaeologists had always believed that cave dwellers were uncivilized people who hit each other over the head with clubs and lacked the "finer feelings" of modern human beings. The paintings proved otherwise, for they showed an appreciation of beauty worthy of any modern artist. Not only that, but the cave painters had gone into a separate chamber to create their works, much as artists today seek privacy. Maria's discovery meant that human beings hadn't changed in some ways over the past 15,000 years.

Professor Vilanova and Don Marcelino wrote letters to journalists in Spain. Maria enjoyed telling the writers how she had found the paintings in the Cave of Altamira, as it became known. The writers nicknamed Maria The Girl of Altamira. For a brief, happy time, The Girl of Altamira and her father were hailed across Spain.

At the time, the leading experts on prehistoric people were in France. For the world to recognize Maria's discovery, the French archaeologists had to approve it. Don Marcelino and Professor Vilanova wrote to them, inviting them to see the remarkable paintings in the Cave of Altamira. Months passed, and not one of the French professors agreed to come.

The problem was that the scientists listened to the famous French archaeologist Emile Cartailhac, who refused to believe the paintings could be thousands of years old. Cartailhac claimed that ancient people lacked the ability to paint pictures as beautiful as those described by Maria's father and Professor Vilanova. He also doubted that cave paintings could last so long, even if protected from the air.

Something else doomed Don Marcelino's claim in the minds of Cartailhac and the other French scientists. They learned that an artist had been working at the Sautuolas' home just before Maria's discovery. He had come to touch up old family paintings, but the French scientists didn't believe that. Without any proof, they accused Don Marcelino of hiring the artist

to paint the cave pictures so that he and his daughter would become famous. Cartailhac and the other scientists were so sure the paintings were fake that they wouldn't even come to look at them.

Now there were more newspaper stories about Maria and her father. No longer were they hailed as great discoverers. Instead, Don Marcelino was called a liar and a faker. The journalists wrote that Don Marcelino had expected Maria to find the faked paintings to fool people into thinking they were real.

Maria's father was deeply hurt by being called a liar. Maria watched his frustration grow as he wrote letters practically begging the professors to visit the cave. His letters went unanswered.

In 1880, when Maria was nine years old, her father published a pamphlet describing the cave and its paintings. That year he went to Lisbon, Portugal, where he passed out copies of his pamphlet at a meeting of archaeologists. But the scientists followed Professor Cartailhac's lead and treated Don Marcelino with *"indiferencia y despredio"* (indifference and scorn), as he later told his wife and daughter.

When Maria's father returned home, his spirit seemed crushed.

Don Marcelino was never the same after that. He often walked about the grounds of his home lost in thought. Sometimes he went out to the cave in the middle of the night to stare at the paintings by candlelight. Although he continued to write to them, most archaeologists considered him "the crazy fellow who faked the cave paintings." As the years passed Don Marcelino lost interest in food, sleep, and life's other pleasures. In 1888, at the age of only fifty-seven, Don Marcelino died. Maria later told her children that the grandfather they never knew had died because of his enormous sorrow concerning the cave.

In 1893 Professor Vilanova died. With the only scientist who had been on their side gone, the cause seemed hopeless. Yet Maria did not give up. She continued to write letters to the archaeologists as her father had done. Maria and her mother also decided that the cave art must be preserved for Don Marcelino's sake. They built a big metal gate to block the cave's entrance. Maria put away the key, vowing

to unlock the gate only when the professors came to clear her father's name. In much the same way, Maria tried to lock the tragic episode of the cave in a corner of her heart, for she did not want it to ruin her life as it had ruined her father's.

Maria de Sautuola grew up to be a lovely young woman. She was a fine dancer and enjoyed the balls and parties that she and her friends and cousins held at their homes. In May of 1895, when she was twenty-four years old, Maria married. Eventually she and her husband had five children. One of them, Emilio Botin, supplied information for this book when he was eighty-three years old.

Almost on the very day that Maria married, four boys discovered cave art in France. More cave paintings were discovered in Europe in the 1890's and early 1900's. Professor Cartailhac and the other French experts finally admitted that prehistoric people were more like us than they had thought. They also remembered "the crazy fellow," Don Marcelino de Sautuola, who had claimed that his daughter had discovered prehistoric cave paintings many years earlier.

Twenty-three years after she had found the cave paintings, Maria received a letter from France. Professor Emile Cartailhac wanted to visit the Cave of Altamira. Would Maria show him the paintings? Maria wrote back that her family had awaited his letter for nearly a quarter of a century.

One day in 1902, Professor Cartailhac visited Maria with another expert on prehistoric caves, the French priest Henri Breuil. Maria, who was now thirty-two years old, removed the key from its hiding place, led the two scientists up the hill to the cave, and unlocked the gate. Just as she had done as a little girl, she held a candle to light the way into the great hall of the cave. Once the professors followed her inside, she looked up at the paintings on the ceiling, as she had done on that summer day in 1879.

It was said that when Professor Cartailhac saw the cave paintings, he fell to his knees in shame. He knew they were thousands of years old because they were similar to the ancient cave art that had been found in France. He also knew that he had wronged an honest man. Professor Cartailhac begged Maria to forgive him

in her father's name. Emilio Botin remembers that, as he was growing up, "My mother told me many times about how the French Professor Cartailhac asked her for forgiveness when he visited the cave." Upon his return home, Cartailhac wrote a famous article called "My Mistake" in which he admitted to the world the injustice he had done Maria's father.

Over the next few years, Maria de Sautuola took her rightful place in history as the discoverer of the first known cave paintings. And the paintings at the Cave of Altamira became known as "one of the seven wonders of the prehistoric world," as one archaeologist wrote. Many people, including Spain's King Alfonzo XIII, came to marvel at the 15,000-year-old paintings and to learn about the girl who found them.

The Girl of Altamira lived to an old age. She enjoyed showing her children and grandchildren the books and articles in which she and her father were mentioned. She also like to tell them bedtime stories. Only instead of fairy tales, Maria told them the true story of how she found the bulls in the cave when she was eight years old.

HOW WERE CAVE PAINTINGS CREATED?

Henri Breuil helped discover how prehistoric people created cave paintings. They made their paints by grinding colored soils into powders and mixing them with animal fats or vegetable oils. Sometimes they blew the paint onto the cave walls and ceilings through hollow reeds. For finer details, they used brushes made of animal hairs.

These tools were used to grind the materials to make paint.

To find their way in dark caves, artists would carry small lamps made of stone. A lamp was about the size of a saucer, and had a fiber wick that burned in animal fat.

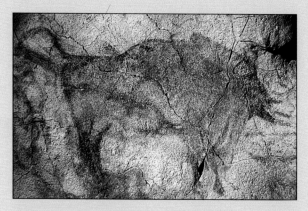

Close-up detail of Altamira Cave's painted ceiling.